CALIGULA

The Evil Emperor Who Proclaimed Himself A God

D.M Alon

Caligula: The Evil Emperor Who Proclaimed Himself A God

Copyright © 2013 by Doron Alon

Published and distributed by: Numinosity Press Incorporated.

Alon, Doron .

Caligula: The Evil Emperor Who Proclaimed Himself A God –1st ed

ISBN: 0-9824722-9-3

Printed in the United States of America
doron@numinositypress.com

Images used for Cover and content:
Cover Created by Shahnaz Mohammed
mailto:NAZNYC@GMAIL.COM
Alexander the Great © v0v - Fotolia.com
Joan Of Arc © Tupungato - Fotolia.com
Ghnegis Kahn © Andrey Burmakin - Fotolia.com
Akhenaten © Travis Hiner - Fotolia.com
Emperor Constantine © Elena Kovaleva - Fotolia.com
Caligula © Aaron Rutten - Fotolia.com
Ancient Jesus Christus Mosaic © philipus - Fotolia.com

http://www.amazon.com/author/doronalon

http://www.interviewswithhistory.com

About The Interviews With History Series

The goal of the Interviews With History series is to provide concise biographical information for people who want to read biographies, but do not have the time to read hundreds of pages or purchase expensive study courses. What you read in an Interviews With History Titles are the pertinent facts; no filler. Written in an easy to understand and conversational fashion. To learn about future releases in this series please visit www.interviewswithhistory.com

INTRODUCTION

Many are the exploits of Rome's Emperors, but few Emperors were as infamous as Caligula. His reign was short, just under 4 years. During that time he wallowed in depravity and lunacy. He came to power with the full backing of the people, but little did they know he would inspire their hatred soon into his reign. Caligula is a fascinating character because he is so complex. What caused his madness? Was he sick with a brain disease? Did he suffer from lead poisoning? Or perhaps he was driven mad by life circumstances. No one will truly know what caused him to act the way that he did.

His upbringing initially was quite good; he was on track to have a good "stable" life. This would all change however as one by one, members of his family die by the vicious hand of the Emperor Tiberius. As he grows up without family members who loved him, he slowly formed his character in this vacuum of affection. A character so maligned and hated that he would go down as one of the most evil people in history. In this volume of Interviews with History, we will cover, ever so briefly, the life of this tortured soul.

CHAPTER 1: CALIGULA'S EARLY CHILDHOOD

Gaius Julius Caesar Augustus Germanicus, also known as Gaius was born in Antium on August 31, 12 AD. He had the good fortune of being born a member of a very prominent family of rulers known as the Julio-Claudian Dynasty. His father Germanicus was the nephew of Emperor Tiberius and was later adopted by Tiberius to be heir to the throne of Rome. Germanicus was one of the most successful Roman generals of his time and was loved by the people and pretty much everyone who encountered him. His good deeds and merciful conduct brought him much love from his troops and even some his enemies. I have heard it said that he was in many ways like John F. Kennedy; people loved him, he was young, charismatic and an overall decent person as far as the people were concerned. It is Ironic that he had a son that would be so wicked.

Germanicus was married to Agrippina the Elder, a feisty and fiery woman who generally spoke her mind with little fear. She often accompanied her husband Germanicus on his various campaigns. She bore Germanicus 9 children, 2 died in infancy and 1 died in his youth. These tragedies undoubtedly created the person she would become.

She was also known to have been raised in a family that sequestered her and so in many ways she let loose when she got older. Their surviving children were Nero Caesar (Not the same Nero who would play the fiddle as Rome burned) Drusus Caesar, Gaius (Caligula), Agrippinna the Younger, Julia Drusilla and Julia Livilla. Their childhood couldn't be more perfect, their parents were successful ambitious individuals and they were all loved by the people.

During Germanicus' campaigns often Gaius would accompany him. Gaius , the youngest of the male children was beloved amongst the soldiers. His mother would dress him up in a miniature soldier's outfit. It is because of his dress that his nickname Caligula was born. The boots the Roman legions wore were called "Caliga". Gaius had his own miniature pair of these boots. Thus, his name, Caligula or "Little Boots". He was so adored that when he was sent to other towns in order to protect him from the fighting, the soldiers would protest. Caligula's presence alone was very much a morale booster for the soldiers. It would seem that from this early start, Caligula would grow up to be a mighty Roman warrior, he was certainly being bred to be.

Unfortunately for Caligula and later for the Roman people, things didn't turn out that way.

Although Germanicus was well loved by the people, he was despised by Emperor Tiberius. Tiberius being a brooding personality was very jealous of Germanicus' fame and viewed him as a rival to the throne. The two were like night and day. Tiberius wanted Germanicus to go away. He therefore sent him on a campaign to Syria .

While there, Germanicus fell ill. In the year 19 AD, he died. The historian Suetonius said that Tiberius had him poisoned. There is little doubt that this is true because Tiberius did not even attend Germanicus' funeral. A sign of disrespect and perhaps guilt. While on his death bed Germanicus told his wife Agrippina that he suspected he was poisoned by the Emperor. Knowing his wife would express her anger publicly, he told her to please keep her hatred and suspicion of Tiberius under control for her safety and for the safety of the children. Unfortunately, she did not heed his words. It was at this point Caligula's wonderful childhood would turn into nightmare. Caligula was only 7.

After Germanicus died, Caligula lived with his mother and siblings. As expected, Agrippina was very vocal about her hatred towards Tiberius and she expressed openly that she wanted to take vengeance on him. This kind of talk alarmed Tiberius and he took drastic measures to keep her quiet. Tiberius knew that he needed to also keep the rest of her family quiet as well. In 29 AD he banished Agrippina and her son Nero to remote islands as punishment for "treason". Nero was forced to commit suicide or to slowly starve to death. Agrippina went on a hunger strike and although they tried to force feed her, she eventually starved herself to death. The other brother Drusus was imprisoned and slowly starved to death. It was said that he was driven so insane with hunger that he started eating the stuffing of his bed.

During this time Caligula and his sisters Agrippina the Younger, Julia Drusilla and Julia Livilla were sent to live with their great grandmother Livia who was also Tiberius's mother. When Livia died in the year 29 AD, they were sent to live with their grandmother Antonia. It was during this time many have thought that he may have committed incest with his sister Julia Drusilla. This rumor, which is most likely true would plague him for the rest of his life. It is also said he had an incestuous relationship with all of his sisters but Drusilla was clearly his obsession. Caligula endured trauma after trauma and in time, this would shape his character. The nightmare of the Roman people was soon to begin.

CHAPTER 2: THE PAMPERED PRISONER

" I am nursing a viper for the Roman people ..."

Several years passed and Caligula was now 19 years old. He was summoned by Tiberius to the Island of Capri where he would spend 6 years of his life. Capri, was an island Tiberius often would escape to in order to indulge in his many perverse pleasures. On Capri, Caligula "Officially" became a man. He shaved his beard, downed special clothing indicating this transition into manhood. But that was pretty much it, there was no pomp and circumstance revolving around this event like there normally would be.

On Capri, Caligula indulged in all manner of lewdness and cruelty. For entertainment, Caligula would watch tortures and executions like we watch movies. He would often frequent brothels and taverns often wearing a wig. Some of his more benign interests were theater , music and dance. Tiberius knew Caligula loved these things and hoped by allowing Caligula to become immersed in theatrical entertainment, it would, in some way, quiet the savage spirit within him. All the while, Caligula was denied any power and this festered in his soul. Despite being mistreated by Tiberius he showed indifference to the fact that Tiberius was responsible for the nightmare of his youth. He knew full well Tiberius was responsible for it. Caligula's handlers tried to coax him into making complaints against Tiberius, but it didn't work. Caligula shrewdly avoided doing so. His seeming indifference was wrongly viewed as passivity. They said "There has never been a better servant, nor a worse master."--Suetonius: The 12 Caesars.

At this time he met Junia Claudilla the daughter of Marcus Junius Silanus, a high ranking member of the Roman Senate and married her. Caligula at this time was chosen to be an Augur or priest. This was considered a very important position but before that was advanced into the pontificate which is a higher order of priest. Unfortunately, his wife died in childbirth. Around this time in the year 37 AD, Tiberius died. Some say Caligula ordered the poisoning of Tiberius and ordered that the imperial ring to be taken off Tiberius's finger while he was still alive. At times Caligula would deny he had any hand in the death of Tiberius, but he did indicate that he wanted to kill him, but out of mercy, decided not to. Knowing what we know about Caligula and Roman Imperial life in general; it is highly probable that Caligula ordered the poisoning of Tiberius, some even said he may have smothered him. It is now that Caligula becomes Emperor of Roman.

CHAPTER 3: IN THE SHADOW OF GERMANICUS

Upon hearing that Caligula was going to be Emperor the people rejoiced. Despite not knowing much about him, the people linked him with the glorious memory of his father Germanicus. They thought that he would be just like his father. Germanicus, however, had leadership abilities; Caligula on the other hand had no formal training and was by no means qualified to be Emperor. But his father's memory casts a halo on Caligula's head. The soldiers remember him as "Little boots" and this affection completely blinded them to the fact that Caligula had no experience whatsoever. Despite Tiberius 's wishes to appoint his grandson Gemellus as co-ruler with Caligula, the Senate pushed that notion aside and made sure Caligula would be the sole ruler.

As a conciliatory gesture, Caligula appointed his nominal co-ruler Gemellus as " Prince of The Youth" and adopted him, thus ensuring he would one day be the ruler if Caligula died. This, of course, was just for show.

At first, Caligula was proving to be a benevolent ruler. He really could do no wrong. Even foreign nations paid homage to him. One of the first things he did was retrieve his mother and brother's ashes and gave them a spectacular funeral. He showed so much respect that he picked up the ashes with his own hands and deposited them in urns. He appointed yearly offerings in their memory. In honor of his father, he renamed the month of September to Germanicus. He honored his grandmother Antonia and promoted his Uncle Claudius from knight to consulship. He added his sisters names to oaths of allegiance to himself. This was a high honor.

He went on to pardon many who were condemned or banished and indemnified against impeachments and past offenses. This won him great popularity. He offered the magistrates of the court free jurisdiction over cases without having to consult with him first. He reinstated the peoples' right of voting in the choice of magistrates. He annulled an unpopular auction tax. He compensated people who lost property in fires. He Restored kings to their rightful places and on top of that he allowed them to collect back taxes and revenues that had accumulated to that point. He was incredibly generous.

For the peoples pleasure he staged wonderful performances in the theaters. He frequently entertained the people with plays of every kind and in several different locations. Some of these performances took place at night . Some said that Rome was illuminated so brightly due to all these performances. He bathed the people with gifts of bread and other valuables.

He ordered performances in other countries. He completed unfinished projects that Tiberius ordered. He likewise repaired temples that were run down. He did all this for the benefit of the people. It looked like the people got what they wished for. A kind and benevolent ruler. Their very own Germanicus. Little did they know that their dear Little Boots, was incubating a monster.

CHAPTER 4: THE CAPRICIOUS BARBARIAN

" Let them hate me so long as they fear me"

In October of the year 37 AD, 6 months into his reign, Caligula became very ill. On several occasions it appeared that he might die. No one until this day really knows exactly what was wrong, but it was clearly a serious illness. All of Rome held vigil for him and many prayed that the gods take them instead of Caligula. Many took dramatic vows to the gods in order to spare Caligula's life. Such vows of course were never really expected to be fulfilled. Under the new Caligula however, such vows were taken very seriously.

As Caligula reemerged from his illness, the people rejoiced, all breathing a collective sigh of relief. They had their little boots back and things could go back to normal. That's what they thought. But it was clear, something was different. Caligula had changed.

The new Caligula was haughty, arrogant and violent. He started to assume grandiose titles such as "The Pious" ,"The Child of the Camp, the Father of the Armies," and "The Greatest and Best Caesar". But that was just the beginning. At one occasion, Kings came to pay their respect. He overheard them talking amongst themselves about who came from a more illustrious royal line. Caligula upon hearing this said, quoting Homer " Let there be but one prince, and one king". It was at this point he was very much inclined to change the entire government structure from imperial to regal. His advisers, however, reminded him that he already outranked any king. At that point he decided that he should then be considered a living god.

In this delusional state he ordered that all the images of the gods have their heads removed and replaced with a bust of his own. He would require people to worship him and make sacrifices to him. Many were forced to refer to him as the most high god Jupiter. This was incredibly blasphemous and was starting to rub people the wrong way. He went on to have a gold statue created of himself in the temple. He made sure that every day the statute would be dressed exactly as he was. Those who were smart realized it would be wise to become priests of his cult and did whatever it took to try to win the priesthood including paying outrageous sums of money in the form of bribes to win it.

On the full moon he would invite the moon goddess to his bed and in his madness imagined that was making love with her. He would have private conversations with the statue of Jupiter and was often heard yelling at the god. Once he was heard saying "If you don't cast me up to heaven, I will cast you down to hell". His religious blasphemy went even further when he had structures built that would connect his palace with the temples of the gods. He so yearned to be in their presence. As he grew weary of Rome, he slowly started detaching completely from his earthly responsibilities.

As a sign of his hatred for humanity and things of this earth he started to disavow his royal lineage by defaming his famous ancestors. He disavowed his grandfather Agrippa saying that he was of "low birth". He took great offense if anyone would rank him amongst the Caesars. He went on to insult his great-grandmother Livia Augusta stating that she too was from lowly origins. This, of course, was not true at all. As for his Grandmother Antonia he disrespected her by refusing all her requests for a private meeting with him. This disrespect was often used as an excuse for her death, but Suetonius mentioned it might have been poison as well. He had no devotion at all, even for the people who treated him well. He went on and forced his former father in law to slit his own throat. As for his uncle Claudius that he promoted from knight to consul was kept alive only so Caligula could make a laughing stock of him.

Caligula: The Lover From Hell

As I mentioned earlier, he had a fondness for committing incest with his sisters, especially his sister Drusilla. In a perverse way he loved her very much and when he fell ill he left her everything in the event of his death. When she married, he would fly off in a fit of jealous rage and would take her from her lawful husband and treat her as if she was married to him. When Drusilla died at the age of 20 , it was clear he was in deep mourning. During the mourning period he banned bathing and laughing. He also forbade dinning with family members. After her death he declared her divinity and would often declare oaths in her name. His other sisters were not so favorable in his eyes. He often referred to them as adulteresses and even forced them to have sex with his male friends. He also accused them of conspiracies against him and eventually had them exiled. Being the Romantic that he was he would often say to his mistresses, past wives and his future wife " This beautiful throat will be cut, whenever I please". Not exactly what most people want to hear during intimate moments.

He would often invite people of noble rank and their wives over for dinner and would run off with the wives in order to rape them. Often he would return to the dinner table commenting on the women's sexual talents further humiliating her , her husband and the guests.

At the age of 27, he meets his soul mate, the flagrantly promiscuous Caesonia; who already had children from another man. She bore Caligula a daughter named after his sister late sister Drusilla. Caesonia had such a bad reputation that many of his advisers found it odd that he would take her as his wife. Despite this, it was quite clear he loved her more than any other wife or mistress he took over his short reign. It was a love that he did not fully understand. He often threatens to have her tortured in order for her to reveal to him why she had such a strong hold on his heart. Again, illustrating his twisted notion of love. Looking back at this union it makes sense. She was after all quite a "free" woman and flaunted her sexuality, this kind of behavior suited him very well since he would often flaunt his own with men and women. He took great pleasure in stripping Caesonia naked in front of his friends. She was so close to him that she was often found riding with him dressed in military clothing with a shield and helmet to boot. Clearly they were meant for each other.

There were some rumors as to whether Drusilla was really his daughter considering that Caesonia was so promiscuous. We will never truly know, but Caligula was convinced that she was his true daughter based on the fact that she had such a wicked temper and would often try to scratch and claw at the eyes of her playmates. It certainly sounds like the kind of child Caligula would bring to the world.

Caligula: An Equal Opportunity Killer

It did not matter who you were, if you were friends or worked closely with Caligula you were not spared humiliation or execution at his whim. He would have distinguished members of society , people of high rank run for miles in their togas as he was riding in his carriage. He would invite people to dinner and had them eat at his feet or served them meat and bread made out of solid gold. Many of these people he had put to death but still continued to send for them as if they were still alive. After a few days he told everyone that they must have committed suicide and therefore could not come to him. When his birthday wasn't publicly announced he fired the people responsible , threw a tantrum and disappeared for 3 days, leaving Rome without a leader.

It did not matter what class you were in, he truly hated all people. While people were claiming their free seats at a midnight circus performance he had them driven away with clubs because he thought they were making too much noise as they took their seats. During this incident many knights and women were crushed to death in the confusion as the people ran for cover.

In the summer, he had a cruel habit of having the curtains removed from the amphitheatre during the hottest time of the day and forced everyone to endure the sweltering heat. If you got up to take shelter you were risking your life. He would often close the granaries so the people would starve periodically. All this without any reason whatsoever.

Events that included wild animals were quite popular in those days and it took quite a bit of meat to make sure the animals were fit to tear people apart. He balked at the expense of the meat and instead, fed them imprisoned criminals. It didn't matter if the criminal was in prison for petty theft or murder, at his whim, he would simply point at a prisoner and have him thrown to the animals for feeding.

As I mentioned earlier, he took the many vows people made quite seriously. While he was sick, one person made a vow that he would fight in the ring with a gladiator if Caligula recovered from his illness. Caligula made sure that this man fulfill his vow. Another man who vowed his own life for Caligula's recovery was killed.

On a whim he had many people of high rank branded on their faces with hot irons and had them work in the mines or fight the wild beasts. If he wasn't entertained by that he would bind them like animals and have them locked in cages and often times had them sawn in half. All this would be done for even the slightest offence. If you looked at him the wrong way you were killed. If you didn't compliment his shows or his "genius" you were tortured and killed. If he didn't like your writing or music you were as good as dead. Caligula himself was bald and so he would have people put to death or have their heads shaved mercilessly for having a head of hair that he envied. He was so self conscious of this that he made it a crime for people to look down upon him, god forbid they witnessed his very bald head. On a rather amusing note, he must have thought he looked like a goat because he forbad people from even mentioning the word goat in any context whatsoever.

In his boundless cruelty he would have the parents of the condemned victims witness their own sons execution and joke with the parents as their sons were being killed. One man who proclaimed his innocence was brought back, Caligula had his tongue removed and then threw him to the wild beasts. His preferred method of execution however was to inflict several small wounds all over the body and would say " Let him feel that he is dying" . He referred to all these unwarranted executions as " Clearing His Accounts". He loved killing so much.

Caligula was just as barbarous and threatening with his words. He would tell people that the one thing he admired most about his character was his inflexibility. When given advice he would scoff and say "Remember That All Things Are Lawful For Me" . He often threatened his exiled sisters saying that the islands are not his only means of punishment, but swords as well; implying he could easily have them killed. He didn't care if people were innocent or not, if an innocent person was executed by mistake, he would proclaim that the person probably deserved it anyway. He truly hated the Roman people and was heard saying " Let Them Hate Me, So Long As They Fear Me". When the people attended games and just happen to root for a gladiator Caligula didn't like he flew off in a rage and said " I Wish All The Roman People Shared But One Neck" .

Caligula thrived off of chaos and destruction. He always lamented that no major calamity took place during his reign as in the past. He often prayed for building collapses, massacres, plagues , famine and other catastrophes. His reasoning was that history would forget a prosperous reign and that only tragedies make the pages of history. Basically, he wanted to be remembered, little did he know he was well on his way to be one of the most memorable and infamous Emperors in history.

His viciousness and cruelty never abated, even in his downtime ,he always had people nearby ready to torture or execute prisoners in his presence. Even on memorable occasions such as the dedication of a bridge he would have people thrown overboard and left them to drown. During an elaborate feast it was discovered that a slave stole small pieces of silver that lined the couches. Caligula immediately had the slave's hands cut off and wrapped around his neck and paraded around the room in front of the guests with a small placard itemizing his crimes. During one very extravagant banquet he suddenly burst into insane laughter. The people near him asked what he was laughing at, perhaps he could share the joke. He looked at them and said " Nothing, it just occurred to me that with the nod of my head I can have both your throats cut". He wasn't the best standup comic.

During practice bouts where gladiators fought with wooden swords. Caligula joined in and was playfully sparring with one. The gladiator fell to the ground purposely. Caligula then drew a real sword and killed the Gladiator on the spot and then pranced around waving the palm branch of victory as if he won a major gladiatorial game. His disrespect for norms goes way beyond games; one time he went to the temple to sacrifice an animal to the gods, he lifted up the ax, paused for a moment and then swung the ax and killed the assistant priest instead.

As I stated earlier, he would often execute people who

happened to look better than he did. He was also jealous of fine writing. Although he wasn't exactly a Homer, Caligula did have some talent. Surely not like some of the greats , but he was no slouch. He did have some talent as a speaker, writer , dancer and in various sports, but he wasn't top notch. Nonetheless he was envious of the great talented men such as Homer, Virgil and Livy . He was so jealous of them he almost had their books banned. He often insulted the integrity of these authors. I guess it would be like going into a British literature class and saying Shakespeare was a mediocre playwright with very little depth. He demolished the statues of great men of history to the point that they could never be fully restored. This envy extended to the law profession as well; he was very close to abolishing the profession altogether.

He didn't spare those great men who were still living. He would strip families and noblemen of their ancient marks of distinction. Tantamount to denying their family seals. He hated other peoples achievements and made sure that he defamed them and disgraced anyone who were more distinguished than him in terms of achievement. One example, he received with honors Pompey, *Cneius,* surnamed the Great, a Roman general and statesman. When Pompey entered the theater , people were bedazzled by him because he had a magnificent purple robe. Caligula, insane with jealousy had him killed.

He Loved The Feel Of Money

Caligula wasn't only outrageous in his personal life he was also completely and utterly outrageous with money as well. Unlike his predecessor Tiberius who was very frugal with Romes wealth. Caligula spent money on such a large scale it shocked even the most decadent of citizens. He made it a habit of bathing in rare and precious oils. He would dissolve pearls of immense value in vinegar and drink them. At times he would literally throw money to the people without care. Although this sounds like a noble and generous act, it was more out of insanity than charity. He built ships and had them encrusted with jewels; installing in them bathes , galleries, saloons and fruit trees. I guess you could say he was the first to build a mega yacht. He would throw lavish parties and dances on them. Sounds similar to what people do now. As today, in that time this kind of ship was considered gaudy and over the top.

Within a year he squandered the entire surplus of Rome. At some point he ran out of money. He had no other choice but to levy taxes. But this was no ordinary hike in taxes. These taxes bordered on the obscene. He knew that taxes would not be popular, so what he did was issue new taxes, have them written down in the smallest possible print so no one could read it. This way he could say that it was public knowledge and that no one could say they didn't know about them.

He used every trick in the book in order to plunder the Roman people. He spared no one and used every malicious device he could think of. He would heap false accusations on people and have their property confiscated. He would annul wills and forced people to make him the sole or joint beneficiary of their estates. If people vowed to make him the sole or at times joint heir to their estates but still lived after making the vow he would consider himself tricked and would poison them in order to collect on the inheritance. During auctions he forced people to bid outrageous sums of money for items not worth the amounts paid. Many of these people were ruined and for some, it was so bad they committed suicide.

He sold everything he could get his hands on; people, both free and slaves. He confiscated the assets of businesses for no reason and sold those too. When he gambled, he always cheated. No one would say anything of course. If they did, they were surely doomed. He went as far as to tax every act of prostitution, both recent and past acts. He taxed individual sexual favors, not just per "visit". Women who were reformed prostitutes had to pay back taxes on all their "jobs" even if it occurred years ago. He even taxed these women after they got married. They needed to pay for every sexual act they had with their own husbands. This back tax applied to pimps and former pimps as well. He turned a wing of the palace into a public brothel and called the patrons " Contributors To The Imperial Revenue". Often he would lend the patrons money at interest for these services. The worst part of this is that he forced women to become prostitutes. It did not matter if she was married or not. These women were being raped and he was making a fortune.

When his daughter was born he claimed that now he had a new burden and fatherhood drove him deeper into poverty. He forced people to contribute to her future and dowry. He demanded that gifts be showered upon him on the new year.

He became so enamored with money that he would often scatter money on the ground and wallow in it, rolling his body over the gold pieces over and over again. He was clearly out of control.

Caligula The Military Man

In terms of military experience, Caligula was not very impressive compared to his father or other Caesars for that matter...But he tried.

Caligula attempted to expand the empire westward around AD 40. He annexed Mauretania which was for all intents and purposes a vassal state to Roman. He at one point invited the Ruler of Mauretania, Ptolemy Of Mauretania to Roman and suddenly executed him. It was believed that Caligula divided Mauretania into 2 provinces but there is still debate about this. In either case it seemed Caligula brought this campaign to be because he was jealous of Ptolemy and Rome was in dire need of funds. Some say it was actually a good move because that region was vulnerable and Caligula may have taken preemptive action to secure the area. It's hard to say which theory is correct. Knowing Caligula, the jealousy seems most congruent. The case is still pending with historians.

Caligula attempted a campaign northward to Britannia, apparently this yielded nothing significant. It is not clear why he went so far north. Some say it was to accept the surrender of a British Chieftain and some say it was simply a training or scouting mission. The historians were especially critical of this campaign because Caligula in his characteristic insanity required people do outlandish things. In his delusion he dispatched letters to Roman as if he conquered all of Britannia.

During his rather fruitless excursions he had the gall to reprimand the people of Roman for enjoying themselves while he was exposing himself to the great dangers of war. But in reality he was under very little threat.

When it looked like he was actually going to go into war, he ordered his soldiers to collect seashells. He looked upon the seashells as bounty from the sea and as a monument to his success he had a huge lighthouse built. He then gave his soldiers a paltry few pieces of gold and made it look like he was exceedingly generous, he says : Go your way, and be merry: Go, ye are Rich". Despite all this he was asked to return to Rome. In anger he returned and blamed the Senate for denying him a victory. In fact there was no real victory to be had in the first place. In a fit, he often threatened to move the capital of the empire since he was so weary of Rome and the senate.

Although his European "campaigns" are the most famous in the historical literature, he was also busy in the middle east. Caligula needed to quell several riots and conspiracies there. This was a tumultuous time. Hellenistic ideas were spreading but they were bumping up against Jewish culture as well. Add Roman law into the mix and these 3 created a powder keg. The High official of Egypt, Aulus Flaccus was no friend of Caligula's. He was loyal to Tiberius , the Emperor that had Caligula's family killed. Caligula had his good friend and Judean Monarch Herod Agrippa go to Egypt unannounced to check on Flaccus. This was a bad move. As Agrippa entered Egypt the Greeks were furious because they viewed Agrippa as the king of the Jews and at that time there was a lot of bad blood between the Jews and Greeks. Flaccus in his haste tried to quell the uprising and the bad blood between Caligula and the Greeks by having statues of Caligula installed in the Jewish synagogues. What a big mistake. This caused citywide rioting. Caligula saw that it was time to get rid of Flaccus for this, and had him removed from office and executed.

Around 39 AD, Agrippa accused Herod Antipas governor of The Galilee as plotting a rebellion against Roman rule. Antipas did confess to Caligula that that was his intention. Caligula had him exiled and installed his friend Herod Agrippa over the governor's territories.

In 40 AD riots erupted again between the Greeks and the Jews. Jews who adhered to strict monotheism refused to worship any image of the Emperor and were maddened by erections of altars to the Emperor. Caligula in spite, ordered that a statue of himself be erected in the main template of Jerusalem. This was by far the WORST thing you can do to the Jewish people, even worse than execution. Caligula was very weary of the Jews. Philo wrote that Caligula "regarded the Jews with most especial suspicion, as if they were the only persons who cherished wishes opposed to his". In fear of civil war, Caligula eventually reversed the order. Probably one of his better decisions during his reign.

Chapter 5: The End Of A Nightmare

"Caligula learned by actual experience that *he was not a god."* - Cassius Dio

24 of January AD 41

Caligula often spent his nights drinking and eating to excess. On the 24 of January he was recovering from one such a night and wasn't so sure he was ready to have dinner but his friends urged him to .On his way he had to walk through various passage ways surrounded by his guards as usual. It was just another day. Caligula however was expecting good fortune because the night before he dreamt that the god Jupiter kicked him out of heaven with his right toe. Left and right had significance in Roman mythology as it does in many religions. Right portending good things and left bad. He thought that the fact he got kicked out of heaven with Jupiter's right toe something good was going to happen. With this in mind he had no reason to believe anything was going to happen to him. Well...He was wrong.

As he walked through the passage ways he encountered an acting troupe preparing for series of events. As Caligula address them, his guard Chaerea cried out " Take That" and stabbed Caligula in the neck. another conspirator stabbed him in the chest. While he lay on the ground Caligula shouted out " I am still alive". So they struck him again, they even stabbed him the genitals. All in all he died of over 30 stab wounds. Upon finding out of this ambush his German body guards rushed to aid and killed some of the assassins, but it was too late. They didn't spare his wife Caesonia, she was killed as well. Insane with hatred they even killed his young daughter Drusilla by grabbing her by the ankles and smashing her brains against a wall.

His body was hastily cremated and what did not burn was thrown into a shallow grave. It was said that his spirit haunted the location of death until he was given a proper burial by his exiled sisters.

People at first did not believe that he was dead, they thought he was just having people say that so he could gauge what people thought of him. But no, it was true. The Mad Emperor was dead.

Caligula was only twenty-nine years old , and reigned for just under 4 years.

CONCLUSION

It isn't clear why Caligula acted the way that he did. But is clear, Caligula was mad, he himself knew he suffered from mental illness. He often mentioned that he needed to leave Rome in order to "clear his head". The question is, why was he like this? When he was a boy he would often have seizures which may indicate that he had what is called " Psychogenic non-epileptic seizures" which in modern day accounts for 20% of reported cases. This makes sense because it is often found in people who have had childhood traumas. He lost many close members of his family and had no social structure to rear him properly. This seizure disorder can also be found in other mental conditions that can often cause the behavior he exhibited as an adult. Mainly, the psychosis, delusional thoughts etc.

He also suffered from severe headaches and insomnia. His insomnia was bad, he was barely able to sleep 3 hours a night and when he did get a full nights sleep, he would often have nightmares or as Suetonius called them "Strange dreams". This certainly did not help matters. Often he would have very high moods as well as crushing lows, this often displayed itself as extreme confidence and extreme timidity, which may suggest bipolar disorder. He was seen roaming the palace at night praying for day light to come. Clearly he suffered from depression. He would often display different personalities and often conducted Roman affairs of state dressed as a woman or as various gods in the Roman pantheon. On the surface one could say that he was just expressing his creativity or perhaps seeing how far he could push people; but it was clear, his behavior was driven by darker forces in his troubled mind. It is also possible he suffered from a disease of the brain.

Another theory that is gaining traction is that he was suffering from acute lead toxicity. Lead to the Romans was considered the father of all metals. The dinner plates, the goblets...everything was made out of lead including the indoor plumbing the Romans were famous for. The Roman aristocracy were very fond of wine and like the Emperors, would drink to intoxication and very often. This consistent and prolonged exposure to lead did have very severe health ramifications. Lead poisoning can explain many of Caligula's issues. His seizures, his faintness, insomnia and behavioral problems can all be caused by lead poisoning. Caligula was not the only one who was studied, other mad Emperors as well were suspected to have lead poisoning, most famously, the Emperor Nero.

One or a combination of these theories may explain Caligula's behavior. I think personally it was a combination of early childhood trauma and lead poisoning. Together they created a toxic environment in his young mind. Despite these theories, the case is still under investigation by historians. Perhaps we will never know why. The secret to his madness may forever be buried in the deep dark recesses of his soul.

About the Author

D.M Alon is the best Selling author of 50 books and founder of Numinosity Press Inc.

He writes on a wide variety of topics including History, Self-help, Self-Publishing, and Spirituality. His conversational writing style and his ability to take complex topics and make them easily accessible has gained him popularity in the genres that he writes for.

To learn more about his other books on a wide variety of topics please visit http://www.doronalon.com or visit his author page at Amazon to find out more.

http://www.amazon.com/author/doronalon

Interviewswithhistory.com

BIBLIOGRAPHY

Suetonius: The 12 Caesars.
Caligula: A Biography
Caligula: Divine Carnage

History's Most Insane Rulers

www.ingramcontent.com/pod-product-compliance
Lightning Source LLC
Chambersburg PA
CBHW071751020426
42331CB00008B/2278